Arthur's Seat
and
Holyrood Park

A Visitor's Guide

C R Wickham-Jones

 HISTORIC SCOTLAND   EDINBURGH : HMSO   SCOTTISH NATURAL HERITAGE

Designed by Derek Munn, HMSO Scotland Graphic Design
Cover picture and principal photography by Stephen Kearney and
Paul Watt, HMSO Photography

© Crown copyright 1996
First published 1996
ISBN 0 11 495746 0

Applications for reproduction should be made to HMSO.
British Library cataloguing in Publication Data.
A catalogue record for this book is available from the British Library.

Contents

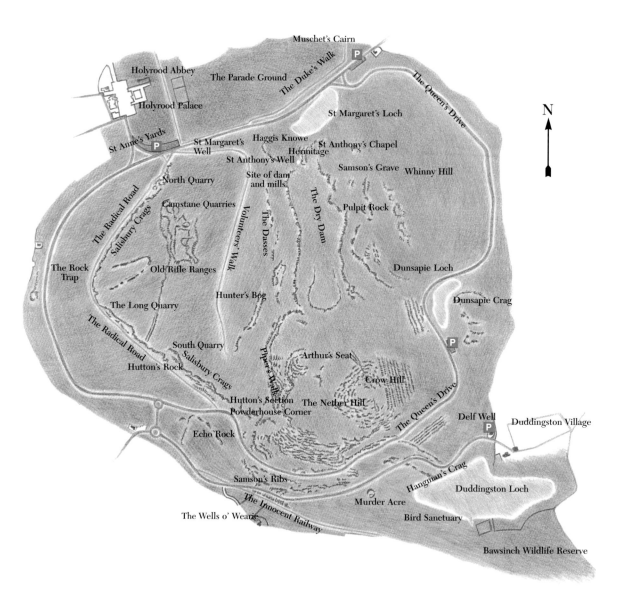

Holyrood Park today with the principal landmarks. Main roads are shown in red, tarmac footpaths in purple.
P *Main carparks.*

Acknowledgements

Research for the writing of this book has taken place over many years. Patrick Ashmore, Mike Scott and the late RBK Stevenson were all very helpful when I first got interested in Holyrood Park. More recently, Mark Collard, Derek Alexander and the Centre for Field Archaeology, Ian Morrison, Alan McKirdy and Caroline Eccles of Scottish Natural Heritage, Elizabeth Wright and the National Museums of Scotland, Ian Armit and David Breeze of Historic Scotland have all taken an interest and helped me out.

Thanks are due for the following photographs: p9: The Natural History Museum, London; p12: Common Rock Rose: Scottish Natural Heritage; p17: Ian Morrison; p18: ©The Trustees of The National Museums of Scotland 1996; p21: Historic Scotland; p22: ©The Trustees of The National Museums of Scotland 1996; pps 23, 29 & 30 By courtesy of Edinburgh City Libraries; p32: both photographs: ©The Trustees of The National Museums of Scotland 1996; p37 By courtesy of Edinburgh City Libraries; pps 42 & 43: Historic Scotland; p53: City Arts Centre, Edinburgh; p55: By courtesy of Edinburgh City Libraries. Map illustration p4 by Heather Insh.

Finally, I should like to thank the staff of HMSO, particularly the photographers who set off up the hill at various times throughout the year and Gillian Kerr who fielded my many queries and requests and kept me on the right track.

Introduction

At the heart of the city of Edinburgh lies Holyrood Park, which contains the craggy mountain known as Arthur's Seat. It is a very special place: there are unusual plants; many different animals and birds; a fascinating geology; archaeological monuments; and an intriguing history.

Today Holyrood Park is a public space. Those who enter may quickly loose themselves among the valleys, lochs, and crags. In the centre of the Park the city can neither be seen nor clearly heard. It is easy to forget that you are within a short walk of the bustling commercial streets of a capital city. This is the magic of Holyrood Park and Arthur's Seat. Few cities anywhere in the world have wild country right at their centre; that is one of the advantages of Edinburgh.

Today Holyrood Park is well known. Every day of the year there are people within the bounds: walking; climbing; or simply relaxing. Even in winter there are always those who wish to take advantage of its peace and tranquillity, and in summer it is very popular. But the Park swallows up its visitors and it rarely feels crowded. Only for certain well-known events, like Fringe Sunday when people gather to sample the music and theatre that help to make up the Edinburgh Festival, does the Park really fill up.

Holyrood Park, with Arthur's Seat, is an important place of relaxation for the people of Edinburgh. It has been so for over one hundred years. Those who use the Park today are merely following in the footsteps of time-honoured tradition. But the history of the Park stretches back well before that and it has not always been a place just for recreation. The Park has seen industry: there were two important quarries within the bounds, and it has seen agriculture: there were several farms and the outlines of many fertile fields may still be made out today. At the same time, it has had strong religious connections: it contained two religious foundations and several holy wells and it was a well-known place of sanctuary. The varied history of Holyrood Park has made it unique. It provides a window onto the rural past. A window that is particularly special because, though it tells of the countryside, it lies at the heart of the city.

Today the Park is designated legally as both a Site of Special Scientific Interest and a Scheduled Ancient Monument. This reflects its great value to both natural and human history. Not surprisingly, its management needs to be undertaken carefully, and this is carried out by Historic Scotland. In order to safeguard the future well-being of the Park the co-operation of all who visit it is needed. This can only be achieved with a good understanding of the particular aspects of the Park that are of interest, and hopefully this book will help to bring that about.

Throughout the history of the Park several themes stand out as of particular interest, and in many cases these themes are still important today. These themes have been used to guide the contents of this book.

(opposite) The view north from the Radical Road.

(below) Arthur's Seat rises above the city trees.

1 The Formation of the Park

The Rocks Beneath

The history of Arthur's Seat and Holyrood Park stretches back into the mists of time, well beyond the arrival of people. To reach a point before the familiar landmarks we have to go back 350 million years, to a time when the climate would have been considerably hotter. In the area of the Park, indeed across the whole of the Lothians, there were low tropical coast lands with lush vegetation. They would have formed a very different sight to that of today.

Even when the hills of the Park first appeared, they would not have been recognisable. They first took shape as a huge volcano,

(opposite) The summit today with the city of Edinburgh and Firth of Forth beyond.

(left) Artist's reconstruction of the Arthur's Seat volcano.

9

which erupted about 350 million years ago, sending clouds of ash into the air and rivers of molten rock (lava) out over the surrounding landscape. This volcano extended many metres above the present summit of Arthur's Seat.

The present summit does indeed mark the heart of the volcano, but anyone standing there today would back then have been deep inside its vent. The volcano was originally twice the height it is today. Erosion, over many millennia, has stripped off its top. The rock of the summit was once part of the pipe of the volcano, and is known as agglomerate. Part of the original cone survives as Whinny Hill, while Salisbury Crags are made up of dolerites that formed deep inside the volcano, from molten rock that never made it to the surface in the original eruptions. Samson's Ribs, too, were formed inside, from basalt that cooled slowly into six-sided columns.

These lavas are particularly hard, they were pushed up from below through the older, softer rocks that surrounded the volcano, and at the same time various ash layers were laid down from above, from the volcanic fall-out.

The volcano would have been active over several thousand years, erupting from time to time, but today it is completely extinct. Hundreds of millions of years have passed since it ceased to be active, and since then it has been eroded by wind, rain, and ice. That which remains today is much smaller than the original mountain, and it has also been tipped on its side by more recent land movements.

The result of all this activity over time is a complex series of rocks of different properties that make up the varied topography of valleys, crags, and summits that we see today.

The Role of the Environment

For much of its recent history the Park has been submerged below a sea of ice. The last glaciation ended about 11,000 years ago, but it was only the most recent of many that have made up the Ice Age, which consisted of a cycle of about fifty colder and warmer periods over the last two and a half million years. During the last encroachment of ice the valleys in the Park were finally scoured out and deepened by the glaciers as they moved across the landscape.

Since the end of the Ice Age the climate has not been stable. Gradually the temperature warmed and vegetation re-colonised the land, but there have been both hotter and colder, as well as drier and wetter, periods since then. The climate is still changing today, but too slowly for us to be much aware of it.

At first life after the ice must have been rather bleak and cold, but things soon warmed up and by 8500 years ago it was slightly warmer than it is today. It is likely that at this time much of the Park was wooded, with boggy, ill-drained valleys. The woodland started to disappear about 6000 years ago when the Stone Age farmers arrived. They needed to clear land for their crops and animals. At first this was a slow process, and even in AD 1128 the area was described as forested in the legend of the founding of the Abbey of Holyrood. Nevertheless, by the sixteenth century, when the Park was divided into sheep farms, the last vestiges of woodland had gone. Some woodland is returning today, for example to the north of Dunsapie Hill, where it has been recently planted. Elsewhere in the Park trees are naturally regenerating.

(opposite) Hard volcanic rocks revealed in the Salisbury Crags quarries.

(below) The grassland in the Park is home to many different species.

(above) Common Rock Rose.

(opposite) In summer, the whin is a spectacular sight.

The vegetation of the Park has changed much over the millennia since the arrival of the first visitors. Walking through the Park today it is easy to have the impression that it is made up of grass alone, but the picture is not quite so simple. Much of the Park is, indeed, grassland, but it includes a variety of types of grassland and these contain many different and interesting plants. The effect of the varied rocks of the Park has been to release different minerals into the soil so that in particular areas specific types of plants may grow. Holyrood Park contains one of the largest and most diverse areas of unimproved grassland in the Lothians. This is all the more unusual for being at the heart of a city. On a walk through the Park the knowledgeable will spot a wide range of species including many flowering plants as well as different grasses.

Originally the lower lands of the Park were marshy and boggy. The name of Hunter's Bog speaks for itself, and recent archaeological work has shown that the area between the Abbey and Salisbury Crags was wet until well into the medieval period. When Queen Victoria and Prince Albert used to stay in Holyrood Palace the Park is recorded as poorly drained and marshy, and this was something that Prince Albert rectified when he included drainage plans in his landscaping of the Park in the 1840s. At this time the lochs of St Margaret and Dunsapie were created.

Most of the original boggy land has long disappeared, but at the southern end of Duddingston Loch an area of marshy ground survives and is incorporated into the Duddingston Loch bird sanctuary. Many wetland species grow here, such as reeds, which used to be cut for thatch. In the Park itself there are other damper areas, such as the mouth of Hunter's Bog or around Dunsapie Loch, and of course these contain a quite different range of wetland and aquatic plants.

The result of the diverse topography and geology of the Park is an unusually varied, rich flora that has been a major factor in its designation as a Site of Special Scientific Interest.

The birds of the Park include both migratory visitors and permanent residents, rare and common species. Many of the birds are typical of more rural areas, such as the Pentland and Border Hills. Both partridge and woodpecker may sometimes be seen, while skylarks add to the enjoyment of a summer's day. An unusual visitor is the fulmar, a sea-bird that has forsaken its usual coastal haunts for the comfort of an inland nesting site. Fulmars nest in quite large numbers on Salisbury Crags, but be warned against approaching too closely: they-spit a foul-smelling oil with great accuracy! Scavengers include crows and jackdaws, and there are also hunters: kestrels; sparrowhawks; and occasionally short-eared owls may be seen.

Finally, to add to the interest of the Park there are, of course, a variety of animals and insects. With so many human visitors, animals tend to be shy and hidden, but the Park is home to many different small mammals such as voles, shrews, and mice. Foxes and hares are also notable, and boxing hares have occasionally been spotted in the Park. Insects include both butterflies and moths, as well as grasshoppers and various species of beetle and fly.

The Human Role

The natural history of the Park makes it a very special place, but human activity has also been influential in shaping it. The Park as we see it today is a relatively recent creation. It has been a "Royal Park" for many centuries, but only recently did it take on the parkland aspect we know today. At the beginning of the nineteenth century it was a much wilder place covered by rough vegetation. There were sheep farms and an un-metalled main route that stretched up across the central craggy ridge, known as the Dasses. Below, lay undrained boggy areas. Queen Victoria and her consort, Prince Albert, used to look out here when they were staying at Holyrood Palace, and it was Prince Albert who instigated its final taming. In 1844, under his guidance, various schemes were drawn up including drainage and the shaping of the lochs, much scrub vegetation was cleared, and the

13

Queen's Drive (first called the Victoria Road) was built. Albert's plans originally extended further, including the building of a rustic restaurant at Dunsapie, but this was finally abandoned.

Naming the Parts

The names of the Park reflect its long and varied history and, not surprisingly, the origins of many of the older ones are shrouded in mystery. It has been suggested that Arthur's Seat, itself, may derive from a Gaelic phrase *Ard-na-Said*: "Height of the Arrows", though there are many other speculations as to its origin. Contrary to popular opinion (or desire), it is not generally held to have had anything to do with the heroic King Arthur.

Holyrood Park is a more recent name, associated with the Abbey, and Palace, that came to govern over it. The Park is also commonly known as the Queen's Park (or King's Park), clearly a reflection of its secular ownership since the Reformation. The name

Salisbury Crags in summer.

of the Abbey is common enough for religious foundations, but here it was apparently derived from the cross (holy Rood) that appeared to David I before its foundation. At the time of the foundation of the Abbey in the twelfth century, the area of the Park seems to have been known as *Craggenmarf*, meaning "Dead Man's Rock", or "Rock of Slaughter".

The Park contains other Gaelic names, for example Dunsapie, meaning "Hill of the wispy grass", but these are mixed with names that reflect the other peoples who have left their mark over the years. Duddingston may have twelfth-century origins meaning "Dodin's Town", but prior to that the settlement seems to have been called Treverlen, an early name which goes back at least to the seventh century. The Guttit Haddie, a distinctive scree slope overlooking St Leonard's has also been known as "The Speldrin". Both names seem to derive from the shape of the feature (like a dried fish), and reflect old Scots influences. Hunter's Bog is a very English name, though it may go far back and refer to the early use of the area.

Many of the more specific names are more recent. Piper's Walk came to be called so when a piper paced the heights in 1778 to keep up the spirits of the mutineers from the Seaforth Highlanders, who were encamped at the summit for three nights. Powderhouse Corner at the south end of Salisbury Crags clearly relates to the quarrying of rock from the Crags and the storage of charges there in the nineteenth century. Volunteer's Walk, down Hunter's Bog, dates from the last century when the volunteers from the Castle came here for target practice.

Finally, there are the names that relate to Prince Albert's vision of the Park. The Queen's Drive and St Margaret's Loch both date to his works. He helped to shape the Park as we know it, but it is also the work of many thousands of others. Nameless people who have lived or worked in the Park over the millennia. They too have left their mark, and it is their contribution that we shall consider in the rest of this book.

2 Human Beginnings

W e do not know who were the first settlers to come to the Park. About nine thousand years ago Stone Age hunters moved across Scotland, making use of the temperate lands revealed by the melting of the ice after the end of the last glaciation. These were the first known peoples of Scotland, but they left little behind them. Their life was nomadic, they moved from place to place in search of animals and plants for food. Their belongings were well adapted to a mobile lifestyle and most of their remains have long since disappeared in Scotland's acid soils. Only the occasional hearth site with perhaps a few holes for tent posts survives to mark their passing, but we do have the stone flakes and blades that they used for knives and arrowheads. One flint tool dated to this time was found on Whinny Hill and shows that the Park was certainly visited by the early hunters.

Other finds of flint tools relate to more recent periods. The Stone Age lasted for several thousand years and incorporated various changes to the way of life. Perhaps one of the greatest changes was the introduction of farming about six thousand years ago and various artefacts relating to the early farmers have been found. So far, no traces of their settlement have been recognised, but a flint knife and arrowhead from near to the summit, and a stone axe from the gateway to Duddingston Church show that they used the Park.

By the Bronze Age, three thousand years ago, human activity in the Park had increased and people had begun to leave more of a mark on the land. A row of indistinct hollows on the Dasses may mark the individual house sites from a Bronze Age village (but it is difficult to date settlements of this type and they may be more

(opposite) The summit and the Nether Hill in their characteristic "lion's haunch" pose.

(below) These broad terraces above Dunsapie Loch are the remains of fields that may have been cultivated as much as 3000 years ago.

recent). Further round, on the hillside opposite Dunsapie Loch is a series of broad terraces that may have begun life as Bronze Age fields, created to provide flat land for crops on the steep slope. To the south of the terraces, in the curve of the Queen's Drive, lie the humps and bumps of past settlement but any early traces here are indistinct due to the remains of a medieval farmstead that lie over them.

The Bronze Age remains also include artefacts. There are more finds from this period than preceding periods, perhaps a reflection of the increasing population that was settling in the area. Towards the end of the eighteenth century a large hoard of bronze objects dating to the Bronze Age was dredged from Duddingston Loch. The Duddingston Hoard included spear heads and swords, all broken, and has been interpreted as the remains of scrap metal to be smelted down in a foundry. Other artefacts, including a bronze sword lying in a bed of charcoal, have been recovered from the slopes nearby, and it is likely that a bronze-smith was working in the neighbourhood, probably sometime round the eighth century BC.

The Duddingston Hoard was found so long ago that the exact details of the find are indistinct, and therefore its interpretation is uncertain. Some accounts refer to remains of timber piles and a possible structure in the loch, others suggest that the find may have had more ritualistic or ceremonial associations. The hoard itself was divided up and given to several different people: including the King, George III; Sir Walter Scott; and the newly formed Society of Antiquaries of Scotland, who used it to found the collections for their museum (now part of the National Museums of Scotland). Whatever the precise nature of the hoard, other metal objects from the Bronze Age have also been recovered from various locations in the Park and a more settled population was clearly developing at this time.

In the Bronze Age we also find the first direct evidence of the early inhabitants of the Park: a burial on Windy Gowl comprising a

Part of the hoard of bronze objects found in Duddingston Loch.

cinerary urn in a stone-lined cist. This was a widespread Bronze Age burial tradition.

The Bronze Age inhabitants of the Park were farmers who lived in small open villages. By the Iron Age, however, life was changing and other emphases were coming into play. The Park contains the traces of four fortifications, and some may date to this time. Throughout the last two thousand years human impact in the Park has been more pervasive and often closely tied to the history of the city that had started to grow nearby.

Duddingston Loch: Archaeological finds suggest that a metalsmith was working on the slopes above the loch about 3000 years ago.

3 Defence and Violence

Two thousand years ago life seems to have been much more unsettled than it had been previously. One possible threat lay in the Romans, who were trying to extend their power in the north. Nevertheless, the invading Roman legions were by no means the only problem. Tensions between different tribes, and even perhaps families, meant that long before the arrival of the Romans most settlements were built inside, or within easy reach of, defences, and this continued afterwards.

The craggy topography of the Park is well suited to fortification and the place-names suggest that this was recognised long back: *Ard-na-Said* – "Height of the Arrows"; *Craggenmarf* – "Dead Man's Rock". The remains of four hillforts may be seen here today. The largest may also be the oldest, that on the backslope of Salisbury Crags. This fort is defined by a low turf-covered bank that runs in a half-moon across the grassy slope behind the Crags; there is no clear sign of internal features such as houses, but it would have been well suited to the protection of cattle as well as local families. The bank does not look like much today, but it would originally have been higher, possibly with a stone or mortar base, and topped by a timber or brushwood palisade.

Also probably early is a smaller and more elaborate fort on Dunsapie Crag. Here waste material from metal-working has been uncovered as well as house sites and midden deposits incorporating domestic rubbish. Behind the Crag, to the east, a small scooped farmstead is connected to the fort by an outlying rampart. This farm

(opposite) The summit and the Nether Hill.

(below) An artist's reconstruction of the fort on Salisbury Crags.

is likely to be Iron Age in date, but it may reflect more peaceful times once the fort had been abandoned (it is described in more detail later on).

To the south, on the rocky outcrop above Samson's Ribs lies another fort in which house sites may be seen. It has not been dated, but a handsome intaglio ring showing the head of Alexander the Great was found here. It had probably been made in the Mediterranean Region in the first century BC, and may well have been brought to Scotland as the personal jewellery of a Roman Officer.

This fine intaglio is of Alexander the Great, from a Roman finger ring found in the fort above Samson's Ribs.

The highest fortification lies round the summit of Arthur's Seat itself. Here there are two stony banks that cut off the gentler approach to the top from the Dunsapie side. These mark the position of the original ramparts, and it is likely that the entrance was in this area, though there is no sign of it today. The banks are low, but they are very eroded and would originally have been much higher, probably with a timber palisade on the top. This would have made an impressive barrier to anyone approaching, and the entrance may well have been more elaborate, with wooden gate towers. Nothing is visible of the interior arrangements, houses and so forth, but some archaeologists think that this fort is more recent, dating to the Early Historic period, 1500 years ago.

With time the threats passed and the forts, apparently, fell out of use. But the Park has not always been peaceful, even in more recent times. In 1677 Murder Acre, to the western end of Duddingston Loch, was the scene of a riot by trades youths who had been barred from a parade organised by the city magistrates on the birthday of Charles II. Soldiers were called in to keep the peace, but before the day ended several youths and at least one onlooker had been wounded and many died.

In 1745 the Jacobite Army camped in the Park, before and after the Battle of Prestonpans, but they did not need to look for fortification and made use of the lower, gentler, slopes above

Duddingston Loch. Debris from the camp, including gun flints and fragments of clay pipes, has been found from time to time, and three skeletons unearthed nearby in 1828 are thought to be the remains of soldiers who died at this time.

In 1778, however, soldiers arrived who were looking for defence. A group known as the Wild Macraas, part of the Seaforth Highlanders who were stationed at Edinburgh Castle, led a mutiny occasioned by the likelihood that they were to be sent out to the East Indias. Conditions at the time were not good, and they preferred to see service closer to home. About six hundred men marched to the summit of Arthur's Seat and a camp was set up in the area of the old, high, hillfort. The people of the city kept them supplied with food and water, and a piper marched above Hunter's Bog playing to keep their spirits up (the origin of Piper's Walk). The encampment lasted for three days and nights before the soldiers were persuaded to come down peacefully, but the tale does not end happily because they were eventually sent abroad, to India, and most died before they could return home.

The high peak of Arthur's Seat is not just a good spot for defence, it is also highly visible and therefore ideal for the siting of a warning beacon. Various beacons have been sited on the summit, the earliest no doubt long before records began: both the Romans and the local Celtic population are known to have used spots like this. More recently, the summit was part of a chain of beacons that stretched along the coast in the eighteenth century as an early warning system against possible invasion. In this century, various guns and anti-aircraft positions were set up around Arthur's Seat and Nether Hill in both world wars. Beacons have also been used for peacetime celebrations, such as Royal coronations, births, and jubilees.

The army has also made use of the Park in other, less troubled ways. In the early nineteenth century it started using the area of Hunter's Bog for target practice, and by

Preparations for a celebratory beacon at the beginning of the century.

1858 there were four rifle ranges running along its base. These were supplemented over the years by various powder houses and pavilions. Although rifle shooting was not initially regarded as more dangerous than archery, there were complaints that the bullets reached the houses of Newington and so the direction of shooting was changed to run from the backslope of Salisbury Crags into the lower side below the summit. The use of the ranges extended up to, and after, World War II, by which time they were also used by civilians: the Edinburgh Rifles Club. Though the shooting has long stopped, and the buildings were all dismantled and removed in 1961, the ranges are fossilised as a modern archaeological trace: various platforms may be seen on the slope behind the Crags when the light is right.

Over the years many other, more individual acts of violence have taken place in the Park. One of the better known occurred in 1720 when Nicol Muschet, a trainee surgeon, finally killed his wife

Hunter's Bog, the tranquil scene of today would have been very different when this area was used for rifle practice.

Margaret, after repeated attempts over the preceding eighteen months. He was hanged for his crime. The murder is commemorated with a cairn near the Meadowbank entrance. This same area was used in 1670 for a duel between a tailor from the Castle and a soldier. Both died: the soldier as a result of the duel and the tailor as a result of his subsequent prosecution and conviction (as a commoner he could not issue the challenge to a duel, a charge he denied).

Many other scenes of violence centre on the dramatic craggy drops: in the eighteenth century a city hangman is reputed to have committed suicide jumping from the Girnal Crag (also known as Hangman's Crag) above Duddingston Loch; and in 1769 the body of Mungo Campbell, who killed an excise officer and then committed suicide in jail to avoid the hangman's noose, was first buried below Salisbury Crags and then hurled from them by the townsfolk.

More recently, in 1972, Salisbury Crags appeared in the news as the murder spot of Helga Dumoulin, a young German girl apparently lured to her death on her wedding night. Her Dutch husband was subsequently convicted of the crime, which seems to have been an attempt to use her Life Insurance as a get-rich-quick scheme.

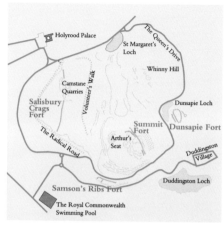

The locations of the fortifications in the Park.

4 A Place of Religion and Sanctuary

By the twelfth century ownership of the Park was divided between the Abbey of Kelso, and the Scottish Royal family. There were a number of small farms within the bounds, but it was also known for its rich hunting grounds. The King, David I, liked to visit the Park to hunt whenever he was staying at Edinburgh Castle. In 1128, on one of these trips, he set out to hunt on a Holy Day, despite advice to the contrary from his priests and advisers. Down in the woods and marshes in the area that is now St Margaret's Loch, he was attacked by a particularly large stag and thrown from his horse. As the King struggled to rise and defend himself the stag disappeared, leaving behind a crucifix formed from a branch of its antlers. That night the King dreamt that he had been called to found an Abbey, and so the Abbey of the "Holy Rood" (crucifix) came into being.

The King made over his lands to the Abbey, and the foundation prospered. The monks made good use of the fertile farmlands of the Park, and also of its waters. They constructed a dam and sluice to control the drainage of Hunter's Bog and in this area they built a mill to grind their grain, though there is no trace of the buildings today, and only a very slight hump is visible to mark the probable position of the dam. They also set up a brewery, lower down by the Abbey. This was to be the first Park brewery in a long tradition that stretches to the present day.

The Park remained in the hands of the Kelso and Holyrood Abbeys until the Reformation in the sixteenth century. During this

(opposite) The ruins of St Anthony's Chapel.

(below) The ruins of the Abbey of Holyrood.

time, a chapel was founded: St Anthony's, on a spur looking out towards the Forth. The exact date of its foundation remains obscure, but in 1426 it needed repairs and the Pope allocated money for these and for vestments. The chapel lay in the part of the Park that belonged to Kelso Abbey, and during the fifteenth century it was a popular place of pilgrimage. The dedication to St Anthony suggests that it may have had connections with a skin hospice in Leith, but there is little to confirm this. Not much is known of its history and in less than two hundred years it had gone out of use: the last record of a chaplain is in 1581. There is a strong tradition that there was a hermitage associated with the chapel, and clear masonry remains in the rock face to the west of the present building have long been noted as its site. Recent examination, however, found no evidence of this and it was suggested that the masonry related to a store house. Little remains of the chapel today, but it is one of Holyrood Park's most romantic relics and much in demand for wedding and other photographs.

The other religious spots in the Park include seven holy wells, most of which have now dried up and disappeared. The most visible and best known today is St Anthony's Well, on the slope leading to the Chapel. The spot is marked by an erratic boulder set in position by the Ice Age glacier, and the bowl is well preserved. Further down, opposite the Holyrood Palace car park, is St Margaret's Well; this used to be known as the Rood Well and the well house in place today was moved from Restalrig in the last century. Other well spots include St David's Well, above St Margaret's Well, and the Delf Well by the Duddingston entrance to the Park.

One result of the ecclesiastical connections of the Park is its position as a place of sanctuary. Though it later became famous as a Debtors' Sanctuary, the right of sanctuary was wider at first. Many different people, from all walks of life, made their way to the Abbey boundary for protection, and this protection extended throughout the Abbey grounds. The early users of sanctuary must have been

St Anthony's Well.

responsible for, or accused of, a variety of crimes. In the early sixteenth century, however, the use of sanctuary for common criminals was repealed, and with the Reformation, Religious Sanctuary was abolished. At this time the Park, newly unified under the Crown, became a Debtors' Sanctuary related to the Royal Palace (debtors were frequently imprisoned at the time).

Holyrood was one of the largest known sanctuaries. The boundary, or Girth, took in all of Arthur's Seat and stretched to the edge of Duddingston Loch. Originally there were other places of sanctuary in Scotland, such as Falkland Palace and Edinburgh Castle, but by the late eighteenth century these were no longer legally recognised.

The earliest recorded debtor to escape his creditors in the Park was a John Scott in 1531; by 1686 there were seventy-five

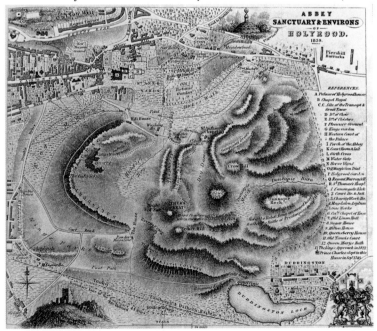

This map of the Park dates to 1839 and shows the boundary of the Sanctuary.

A contemporary view of the tenements in which the Abbey Lairds could rent accommodation.

people and by the nineteenth century there was a well-established system, in 1816, 116 people were living in Sanctuary. Those who entered the Sanctuary were known as the Abbey Lairds. After twenty-four hours, they had to apply to the Baillie and pay an "entry fine" in order to set up residence. Most lived in the area round the present Palace, then known as St Anne's Yards. Here, in the old buildings once used by the aristocracy at Court, a township of tenements had sprung up where rooms could be rented for between three and six shillings a week. Life was strictly controlled: there was a complex internal law system relating to criminal offences, debt incurred in Sanctuary, and the problem of people being lured out by their creditors. This was administered through the Baillie, and the community at St Anne's Yards even included a prison! It is reported that the Lottery did well inside the Sanctuary.

Those in the Sanctuary could leave for twenty-four hours a week, on the Sabbath, without jeopardising their position, and many used this to attend to regular business, buy food, and mend their affairs. One minister would leave early to walk to Corstorphine and back so that he could continue to preach! Within the Sanctuary

30

there were people of all backgrounds, renowned people of the day mixed with more humble folk. Thomas de Quincey, a well-known writer, composed several works from his home there, and even Sir Walter Scott thought he might have to make use of it (weighing up the relative merits of the Isle of Man and Holyrood Park, but luckily he had to make use of neither). Even royalty was not exempt: the future Charles X of France stayed in the Palace to avoid his creditors for over two years, from 1796 to 1798, and brought many courtiers and servants with him.

Once their finances improved, people could return to normal life. The population of the Sanctuary was constantly changing and provided a source of curiosity to their fellow citizens of Edinburgh. It is said that those within the Sanctuary were expert at recognising newcomers who would be instantly placed in one of three categories: tourists come to stare; creditors come to look for "their" debtor; and new debtors arriving to seek safety.

Over time the laws relating to debt were changed and imprisonment fell out of use. So, the use of the Sanctuary was gradually abandoned and by the end of the nineteenth century it had fallen into disuse. The last recorded inhabitant was an Edinburgh solicitor: David Bain in 1880. Today there is no sign at all of the thriving, if eccentric, community that made up the Abbey Lairds. The area of tenements lies under the present Palace gardens and car parks, and even the tradition of sanctuary has been forgotten by most people.

One quirk of the sanctuary rights of Holyrood Park, however, is that they were never repealed. It is said that the Park is still a place of sanctuary for debtors and the office of Baillie still exists, though whether the modern system and organisations such as the Inland Revenue would take a benign eye of our old rights and traditions seems doubtful.

Not surprisingly, with all of its inhabitants, the Park has often been used for burial. Both the Abbey and St Anthony's Chapel had

OR, EDINBURGH POLITICAL AND LITERARY JOURNAL.

XX. NO. 1724.   SATURDAY, JULY 16, 1836.

STRANGE DISCOVERY.—About three weeks ago, while a number of boys were amusing themselves in searching for rabbit burrows on the north-east range of Arthur's Seat, they noticed, in a very rugged and secluded spot, a small opening in one of the rocks, the peculiar appearance of which attracted their attention. The mouth of this little cave was closed by three thin pieces of slatestone, rudely cut at the upper ends into a conical form, and so placed as to protect the interior from the effects of the weather. The boys having removed these tiny slabs, discovered an aperture about twelve inches square, in which were lodged seventeen Lilliputian coffins, forming two tiers of eight each, and one on a third just begun! Each of the coffins contained a miniature figure of the human form cut out in wood, the faces in particular being pretty well executed. They were dressed from head to foot in cotton clothes, and decently "laid out" with a mimic representation of all the funeral trappings which usually form the last habiliments of the dead. The coffins are about three or four inches in length, regularly shaped, and cut out from a single piece of wood, with the exception of the lids, which are nailed down with wire sprigs or common brass pins. The lid and sides of each are profusely studded with ornaments formed of small pieces of tin, and inserted in the wood with great care and regularity. Another remarkable circumstance is, that many years must have elapsed since the first interment took place in this mysterious sepulchre,

and it is also evident that the depositions must have been made singly, and at considerable intervals—facts indicated by the rotten and decayed state of the first tier of coffins and their wooden mummies, the wrapping cloths being in some instances entirely mouldered away, while others show various degrees of decomposition, and the coffin last placed, with its shrouded tenant, are as clean and fresh as if only a few days had elapsed since their entombment. As before stated, there were in all seventeen of these mystic coffins; but a number were destroyed by the boys pelting them at each other as unmeaning and contemptible trifles. None of the learned with whom we have conversed on the subject, can account in any way for this singular fantasy of the human mind. The idea seems rather above insanity, and yet much beneath rationality, nor is any such freak recorded in "The Natural History of Enthusiasm." Our own opinion would be —had we not some years ago abjured witchcraft and demonology—that there are still some of the weird sisters hovering about Mushat's Cairn or the Windy Gowl, who retain their ancient power to work the spells of death by entombing the likenesses of those they wish to destroy. Should this really be the case, we congratulate the public, but more especially our superstitious friends, on the discovery and destruction of this satanic spell-manufactory, the last, we should hope, which the "infernal hags" will ever be permitted to erect in Scotland!

their own burial grounds. Archaeological work round St Anthony's Chapel has uncovered a number of burials in the narrow strip of ground to the north. They were probably city folk and others who wished to be buried close to the Chapel. In the sixteenth and seventeenth centuries victims of the plague were lodged in specially built huts in the Park, a doctor was appointed to attend them, and they were buried there when they died. More recent burials are suggested by the three skeletons uncovered near to Duddingston in the last century: they probably date from the time when the Jacobite army camped in the Park in 1745.

Nevertheless, by far the best-known Park burials did not involve bodies at all. In 1836 five schoolboys discovered a small, carefully protected, cave high on the slopes below the summit. Inside were two rows of tiny wooden coffins each containing a little wooden figure. The figures were carefully carved and dressed in funeral clothes, and the coffins were elaborately decorated with pieces of tin. The boys played with their find and several coffins quickly disintegrated, together with their occupants, but eight survived, to be shown to a school teacher and reported on by *The Scotsman* of the day (Saturday 16 July 1836). At first they were kept in a private museum, but finally they were donated to the museum of the Society of Antiquaries of Scotland, now part of the National Museums of Scotland, where they are still an item of great curiosity.

Even today, there is no clear explanation for this mysterious find and speculation as to the origins of the coffins is rife. At first it was thought that they had been laid to rest over a period of time, because the lower coffins were quite decayed, while the upper ones were in better condition, but this was probably because of the damp ground conditions. Recent tests have shown that they are all close in age. The coffins, themselves, are made of Scots pine, and it has been suggested that the figures were adapted from a set of wooden soldiers. Each is carefully and individually dressed, and it is hard not to speculate that each was intended to represent an individual, living, person.

In its original article, *The Scotsman* reported the commonly held belief that the coffins relate to the "infernal hags" of the Park, and had been buried for some black magic purpose. This is still a popular explanation, but others have been put forward, including that they may relate to gypsy burials, or that they represent the burials of people who have died at sea or abroad. Two recent investigators have suggested that they may have been buried by someone as token burials for the victims of Burke and Hare (who sold seventeen bodies for dissection), and they certainly date from the right period.

It is unlikely that we shall ever know the true explanation behind the seventeen little coffins and their smartly dressed occupants. But we can be sure that they will remain some of the best known, if elusive, inhabitants of Holyrood Park.

Finally, it is worth noting that though there is no longer a church within the Park, its religious associations have not completely disappeared. At Easter people gather to roll pace eggs (colourfully decorated, hard-boiled eggs) down the slopes, and every May Day several hundred people climb to the summit to attend a service of Christian worship as the day breaks. These are both manifestations of ancient traditions. Egg rolling is an ancient Easter custom, and May Day was once the Festival of Beltane, an important event in the Celtic year. Traditionally, on this day, people would gather at sunrise to bathe their faces in the dew. This tradition is still associated with Arthur's Seat, and the Christian service is a popular continuation of a festivity that is centuries old.

(opposite and below) Some of the tiny coffins found near to the summit in 1836.

5 A Royal Park

The place-names and traditions of the Park confirm its Royal associations, and royalty has indeed played an important part in shaping it as we see it today.

Prior to David I and the foundation of the Abbey of Holyrood, the Park was a favourite hunting spot for the King and his court when they were stationed in Edinburgh Castle. It must also have provided a small amount of revenue from the rents of the agricultural tenants who farmed the various small farms. In 1128 David made over his lands to the Abbey, but the royal connections did not stop. The Abbey buildings included a guest house and over the years, as the Castle was not always large enough for the royal guests, its facilities were increasingly used by guests from the court. In the early sixteenth century its facilities were developed by James IV and subsequently by James V, for the use of the royal household, and it was natural that they should become increasingly important on the annexation of the monasteries in the late sixteenth century.

Prior to the annexation the Park was unified for the first time when, in 1541, James V built a wall to enclose the whole area. Afterwards, not surprisingly, the Palace become one of the principal royal residences. It did not, however, take on its present form until the late seventeenth century, when it was remodelled under Charles II.

Mary, Queen of Scots, is particularly associated with Holyrood Palace in its early days. She stayed at the Palace when she was in Edinburgh, where she conducted both business and pleasure; and where she was witness to the murder of her secretary David Rizzio in 1566. Despite the troubled times, she also made use of the Park

(opposite) A view from the Park over north Edinburgh. In the foreground lies the Palace of Holyrood and the area of St Anne's Yards where the debtors' tenements once stood.

for recreation. In 1562 she arranged elaborate festivities to celebrate the marriage of one of her ladies-in-waiting: the land of Hunter's Bog was flooded and model ships were used to create a miniature naval pageant based on the siege of Leith which had taken place in 1560.

During Mary's days the Park was also the scene of aggression throughout the wars between her and the supporters of James VI. It provided the ideal location for various skirmishes and ambushes, and on 10 October 1571, James VI's supporters sited two small cannon on Salisbury Crags to bombard the Old Town. It was not a successful venture and one of the cannon exploded. Eighty years later Scots Musketeers used the Park to fire on Cromwell's troops as they advanced from Leith in 1650.

Bonnie Prince Charlie also used the Palace and Park, though not for long. By his time the Palace had been remodelled, and the new long gallery was particularly suited for formal gatherings: assemblies and dances were held here during his residence in 1745. The Park provided suitable terrain to station his troops on their brief encampments in the neighbourhood. Before his time the Park had

St Margaret's Loch: formed as a part of the nineteenth century improvements made by Prince Albert.

also been used as grazing, to provide pasture for the Cavalry horses from the 1650s to 1711. Occasional thefts of individual chargers meant that this was not without its problems.

A century later Queen Victoria and her consort Prince Albert came to be particularly fond of their stays in the Palace. At first they looked out over a Park that was largely wilderness, the land behind the Palace is described as being both marshy and smelly. The common sewers emptied out on to the land at the foot of the Crags, and in 1838 Courtoy and Macmillan called this area "most odiferous", in their *Guide to the Chapel Royal and Palace of Holyroodhouse*. Prince Albert spent much time drawing up plans to improve the situation, and in 1856 he put into action his ideas to landscape and improve the Park. It was at this time that it took on its present form: the Queen's Drive, first called the Victoria Road, was built; the Palace gardens were improved; the marshes were drained; and St Margaret's Loch and Dunsapie Loch both created. Originally, Albert's plans went further. He also wanted to build a rustic, thatched restaurant at Dunsapie, but this inspired a flurry of angry letter-writing to *The Scotsman*, and the scheme was dropped in the face of strong opposition.

The nineteenth-century improvements also took in the flat ground between the Palace and Meadowbank. In the early nineteenth century this comprised various gardens and orchards, and belonged to different proprietors, including Lord Haddington and the Duke of Hamilton. By the 1850s, however, it was open land, known as "the Parade Ground". In 1860 this area was used for a review of the troops: the Royal Volunteer Review, an elaborate occasion that involved several regiments. There was a grandstand for 3000 of the most important spectators, others climbed

A religious meeting in the Park c.1905.

the slopes of Salisbury Crags, and the whole area was crowded with flags and tents. Over a hundred thousand spectators took part that day. Twenty-one years later the spectacle was repeated, but in rather different circumstances. The Review of 1881 has come to be known as the "Wet Review" on account of its torrential rain. The Scottish climate can rarely be trusted and this time few of the spectators stayed until the end.

The Parade Ground is still important, both for Royal events and more ordinary ones. In 1977 the celebrations for Queen Elizabeth II's Silver Jubilee took place there, and it is currently the site of Fringe Sunday, one of the most important annual gatherings of the Edinburgh Festival.

(below and opposite) Fringe Sunday, one of the highlights of the Edinburgh Festival when many artists and performers are attracted to the Park.

6 Living and Farming in the Park

Though the Park may now seem abandoned, over the millennia it has been a home to many, not only its Royal visitors. Early maps and illustrations provide evidence of many buildings, both houses and others, and it is clear that it did not always have the pure countryside aspect of today. Previously the Park must have been a favoured place for settlement; with its abundant supplies of sweet water, fertile soils, easy access, and yet high crags for defence when necessary. It is more of a surprise that all settlement has now gone.

The earliest remains of houses, the row of hut circles on the Dasses, are not clear except to a trained eye. This small village may date back as much as 3000 years, and we know little about it. Of the later remains some are obvious while others are semi-hidden, blending well into the rocks and vegetation. From the Iron Age onwards settlement in the Park seems to have increased, but with the exception of the fort above Samson's Ribs there is little trace of the houses and outbuildings that once sheltered behind the various defences. However, there is one farmstead that remains from this time: a small settlement on the backslope of Dunsapie Crag.

The Dunsapie farmstead lies on the eastern slope of Dunsapie Crag, below a large erratic boulder. Here, a hollow about 21 metres (70 feet) across has been dug and inside the remains of at least five circular platforms have been recorded by archaeologists, though only two are easily visible. These platforms mark the position of house

The slopes opposite Dunsapie Loch in winter. Five hundred years ago this hillside was the site for one of the main farms in the Park.

Haggis Knowe, these terraces are some of the old field remains that occur throughout the Park.

*An artist's reconstruction of the small
scooped settlement on the back of
Dunsapie Crag.*

floors, though we do not know whether they were all in use at the same time, nor for what purpose each was built. On the downhill side of the settlement there is a bank, broken by a clear entrance, and another bank curves uphill around the outside. The settlement is connected by these banks to the fortifications round the top of the crag and it was probably occupied at about the same time that the fort was in use, perhaps as life became more peaceful so that people could move out once more from behind their defences.

The Dunsapie farm is a typical "scooped farmstead", inside there would have been a round-shaped dwelling house, alongside at least one outbuilding or byre, and the outer bank may have been topped by timber or thorn brush, as much to keep marauding animals out, as stock in. Below the farmstead and towards Meadowbank are the faint traces of several terraces, probably the fields cultivated by the inhabitants of the farm some two thousand years ago.

For many centuries after the Iron Age the physical record of the ordinary inhabitants of Holyrood Park is lacking. The monks of Holyrood and those of Kelso had agricultural tenants, but it is impossible to identify with certainty any of the dwellings relating to their activities. There are, however, plenty of remains relating to the later inhabitants and it is likely that these may mask some of the earlier sites. Farms, after all, tend to stick to the same fertile spot.

One of the largest and most interesting groups of settlement remains lies above Duddingston, on the slopes above the bend of the Queen's Drive. Here the position of two medieval farmsteads is marked by a series of long house platforms, and fainter rounder scoops suggest that they overlay the site of a group of prehistoric round houses. Above and to the side of this settlement, a series of well-developed terraces covers the slopes rising towards the summit. These are grass covered today, but some five hundred years ago the visitor would have seen a very different scene. At that time they would have been ploughed fields, providing crops for the farmers and their landlords.

Cultivation terraces occur at various spots through the Park and they may go back in use well before the medieval period. Elsewhere in Scotland they have been shown to date back to the Iron Age. Whatever their origin, the vision of the plough-team with oxen, ripening grain, and busy harvest activity is a very different one to the grassy peace of today.

The remains of other fields may be seen on the lower slopes as broad banks or rigs. These, too, mark the sites of ancient ploughing, but on flatter land. They are particularly well preserved in the Prestonfield golf course. In some cases they curve in a reversed "S" form towards the end of the bank, this has arisen where the plough-team swung round before changing their direction to go back down the field. Holyrood Park was clearly a fertile place when James V enclosed it in the sixteenth century. This was a time of great change, and not only of landlord: contemporary economics meant that cultivation was soon to disappear. Sheep in large numbers were introduced to the land, and another type of farming took over. In the 1540s the terraced fields were still in use, but within a decade or so they lay abandoned and the Park was divided into five major grazing zones. The last record of tillage in the Park is in 1610.

An artist's reconstruction of life in the medieval farmstead above the Queen's Drive.

A view of the old terraced fields opposite Dunsapie Loch as they are today.

The grazing zones were still rented out, and throughout the Park there are various house sites that may represent the homes and bothies of the shepherds. One of these lies on the Dasses, below the hut circle village, another is beside the Dunsapie carpark, and a third lies near St Leonard's, just below the Queen's Drive as it curves up towards Dunsapie. One of the Park's most famous fictional inhabitants, Jeanie Deans lived in this area. The character of Jeanie Deans was created by Sir Walter Scott, but he not only based her story on fact (the life of Helen Walker from Dumfries), but also used an existing cottage situated at St Leonard's in which to house her.

With time the herd's cottages fell out of use and into disrepair. They were probably never very substantial and today only their grass-covered floor platforms survive. The number of sheep in the Park also gradually declined, but they were not finally removed until 1977, by which time they were regarded as a hazard to the increasing amount of traffic. This marked the end of the Park's days of agriculture: only the broad terraces and lower rigs together with faint house sites remain as witnesses to the days when the air would ring with the sound of the plough-teams and the cries of children and dogs.

The last Park shepherd lived on the south side, where there stands a group of cottages known as the "Wells o' Wearie". As the name suggests there is group of wells associated with these cottages and they were originally used by local women to wash clothes. The clothes would be bleached and spread out to dry on the nearby hill slopes, but in 1845 this practice was stopped because it was felt that it conflicted with the increasing public use of the Park for recreation.

Recently, the only people to live inside the Park, apart from the residents of the Palace, have been those who occupied the Lodges at the various entrance gates. Today even their number is down: the Lodge at the Palace entrance was converted in the 1980s for use as a visitor centre with an exhibition area. Today it is closed.

(opposite) A view of Dunsapie Loch, created during the improvements carried out in the nineteenth century under the guidance of Prince Albert.

A Place of Work: Industry and Scholarship

The industrial uses of the Park stretch back in time, though they took place on a scale much smaller than that of most industry of today. The early inhabitants doubtless practised various crafts, but left almost no trace of these: debris from metal-working, including a sandstone mould to cast rings has been discovered inside the hillfort above Dunsapie.

Over one thousand years later, the monks of Holyrood used the local waters for brewing and they set up a dam and mill at the entrance to Hunter's Bog for the grinding of grain, but there is little physical trace of their activities today. Nevertheless, the tradition of brewing was one that continued for many centuries. Scottish and Newcastle breweries are still active in the Canongate and, being a close neighbour of the Palace and Abbey, could be said to have followed directly in the footsteps of the monks. On the other side of the Park, the Park Brewery, built by Ushers in 1860, was subsequently used for the distillation of whisky, though it has now closed.

Other industry was more destructive than the brewing. The unique geology of the Park, with its combination of hard volcanic rocks and softer sedimentary rocks, made it particularly valuable as a source of building stone. There are several major quarries in the Park which have left clear traces. On the backslope of Salisbury Crags lie the Camstane Quarries, where a soft sandstone was

(opposite) The remains of the Camstane Quarries show up as a clear scar on the backslope of Salisbury Crags.

extracted. The deep quarry pits are clearly visible and make an interesting spot to explore and observe plants and wildlife. Leading up to them from the entrance to Hunter's Bog is a worn hollow way. The depth of this sunken track, worn over the years by the passage of many well laden carts, is a mute testimony to the extent of the quarrying activity. Though it is now grass covered and rural, it is not hard to imagine the squeaking of the cart-wheels and the cries of the drivers as they urged their animals on.

The date of origin of the Camstane Quarries is uncertain, but they may have been used in the construction of Holyrood Palace between 1529 and 1536, and they seem to have been out of use by the 1850s. The stone had a variety of purposes for paving and building, and one of its last uses was for the construction of the Piershill Barracks.

There were other small quarries inside the Park, but by far the greatest activity took place along the front of Salisbury Crags, where the hard volcanic rock, known as Dolerite, was exploited. The extraction of this stone stretches back: in 1666 it was well enough known to be exported to London for street paving. The quarrying took place under the auspices of the Keeper of the Park, Lord Haddington, and for many years it proceeded without controversy. Though there was much demand for the stone, extraction was limited by the technology of the day. However, at the turn of the nineteenth century the introduction of new techniques involving the use of explosives allowed work to speed up. It is estimated that about 100 tons of material were being extracted per day (up to 36,000 tons annually), and public alarm was raised as the well-loved outline of the Crags began to be eaten away. In 1819 an action was raised against the Earls of Haddington to stop the destruction. Not surprisingly, it was some time before matters were resolved, but in 1831 the House of Lords ruled that Lord Haddington had no right to remove stone from the Park. Work stopped, and in 1845 the 9th Earl of Haddington was paid over £30,000 for the surrender of his office of Park Keeper to the Crown. Today it is possible to enter the quarries from the Radical Road. Large blocks lie abandoned, as they must have been when the 1831 ruling took force.

Access to the quarries of Salisbury Crags was originally effected by a rough track which skirted the base of the Crags. In the 1820s this pathway was improved by the building of the Radical Road. In keeping with the increased use of the Park for recreation, the Radical Road was not intended for industry, but rather as a route for pleasure and inspiration. It was conceived by Sir Walter Scott together with various friends, and set up as a scheme to employ unemployed weavers from the west of Scotland. The path they created quickly became popular and the weavers left more than the physical reminder of their time in Edinburgh: their radical politics are remembered in the name of their path – the Radical Road. Ironically, the application of hard work was originally intended to lessen their radical views, not enshrine them in history.

Originally, it was intended to plant the base of the Crags along the Radical Road with exotic flowers and shrubs from overseas, in order to increase public enjoyment of the walk. Permission was denied, however, by the Keeper of the Park, Lord Haddington, because he feared increasing vandalism and a detrimental effect on his quarries and agricultural tenants if public access were to be dramatically enhanced.

Surprisingly, though it is now a place of peace and tranquillity, the cessation of quarrying was not the end of industry within the Park. 1831 saw the ending of quarrying, but in the same year one of Scotland's first freight railways opened and it just clips the Park. The line ran from Dalkeith to St Leonard's, and was built to carry coal into the city from the Dalkeith mines. Originally, the freight was horse drawn and thus it earned its nickname: "The Innocent Railway", horse-drawn carriages were considered by many to be much safer than the newfangled steam engines which encompassed all sorts of supposed dangers. The Innocent Railway was quite a feat

(opposite) Hard volcanic rocks from the quarries on the face of Salisbury Crags were much in demand for paving slabs and building stones.

(below) Salisbury Crags in winter. The Radical Road may be seen, winding up towards the old quarry sites.

of construction: it included a stone tunnel; a cast-iron bridge; and a timber viaduct. Though it was designed for freight, the railway was soon popular with passengers, so much so that the company quickly added passenger coaches converted from a variety of ordinary road waggons. Eventually, locomotives took over from the horse-drawn rolling stock, and the line continued in use into the 1960s. Today, the route is used as a cycle path and public walk-way.

The use of the Park as a place of work has not always involved large-scale disturbance. The geology is such that it was a particularly important place for early geologists. As much as 200 years ago it played a significant role in the debate on rock formation and early volcanic studies. One of the best-known scholars was James Hutton, a geologist of the eighteenth century who was deeply involved in the controversies of the day, surrounding the origins of the earth. Hutton spent much time studying the rocks of Salisbury Crags as they were freshly revealed during quarrying. He used his observations to illustrate his theory that igneous rocks were formed from hot, molten rock which had been pushed up between older material and subsequently cooled and solidified. The phenomena observed by Hutton are still visible in the quarry face that he studied. The original rock face, or section, where he made his observations was quarried away in the 1820s, but the same phenomena may still be seen in the face behind. Today it is known as Hutton's Section and it is visited by geologists from all over the world.

Hutton knew the quarries well, and recognised the scientific interest of the rocks. He is reputed to have asked the quarry-men to preserve one upstanding outcrop of rock because it showed a particularly good example of a vein of iron ore running through the stone. This outcrop is known as Hutton's Rock and it still stands today at the entrance to the quarry; it must be one of the first examples of conservation in Scotland.

Hutton has not been the only academic to study the Park. Throughout the nineteenth century it provided much of interest to

(opposite) The rock faces reveal different types of rock that are still of interest to geologists who wish to study how the volcano pushed its lavas (below) through the older sedimentary rocks (above).

(below) Hutton's Rock, saved from quarrying at the end of the 18th century, it is one of the first examples of conservation in Scotland.

geologists, botanists and naturalists and it is still a well-used educational resource. The varied topography has also meant that it is a great training ground for surveyors and map-makers. In the last century surveyors came not just to make plans of the Park, but also to try out new equipment and techniques. In 1855, the Royal Engineers came to the Park as part of a project to calculate the weight of the earth and the gravitational constant. This involved very detailed mapping, plus astronomical observations from the summit and other spots. Because of the irregular shape of Arthur's Seat they constructed a three dimensional model of wood which could be used to calculate the volume of rock in its different zones. The model (at a scale of 1:1056, or 60 inches to 1 mile) may be seen today in the Royal Museum of Scotland.

Today the number of specialists interested in the Park has been swelled by archaeologists, a relatively new science. One aim of this book is to demonstrate the great archaeological interest and large number of remains in the Park, but the archaeologist's task is never done. New sites and information are being discovered all the time, both by erosion, and by accident as the sun casts a new shadow on some stones, or sheds greater light on a previously unknown spot.

The rocky terrain of Holyrood Park is a regular training ground for students of all disciplines from various departments in the different universities of the city. In addition, groups of school children are frequently to be seen taking advantage of their local open-air classroom.

8 Inspiration and Recreation

There is no doubt that over the years the crags and valleys of Holyrood Park and Arthur's Seat have brought relaxation and inspiration to many. Queens, holy men, and scholars have all loved and frequented the rocky glens, as well as artists and townsfolk. Of course, the majority of the Park's visitors have passed without record, but some have left a more lasting trace.

Many artists have found inspiration in the magnificent views out over the city and across to the Forth. These include Hugh William Williams (1773–1829). The Park has also appeared in novels: Sir Walter Scott set the story of Jeanie Deans among the

Edinburgh from Arthur's Seat, *by Hugh William Williams (1773-1829)*.

shepherds' cottages of the nineteenth century in *The Heart of Midlothian*, and this book contains some evocative descriptions of the Park. In *The Private Memoirs and Confessions of a Justified Sinner* author James Hogg uses Holyrood Park to site some of the book's events, and a young Edinburgh student, Sir Arthur Conan Doyle, was inspired by his daily walk to University past Salisbury Crags for the setting of his novel *The Lost World*. In the 1920s and 30s St Leonard's Hall, just outside the Park, was occupied by a girls' school, St Trinnean's, reputedly the inspiration for the *St Trinian's* stories of Ronald Searle whose niece was one of the pupils.

Poets, too have left their mark. There are many traditional songs and verses that make use of well-known Park landmarks. In the seventeenth century Robert Fergusson wrote about St Anthony's Well. The Wells o' Wearie have been a popular topic, and more recently William McGonagall took the Wet Review of 1881 as inspiration for his poem *The Royal Review*.

Over the years the recreational use of the Park has grown. Today, it seems dominant, but even in the early years of the nineteenth century there was increasing concern at the great number of visitors in the Park. In the 1820s Lord Haddington was worried by complaints of disturbance to the sheep by his agricultural tenants, but by 1845 the point of view had shifted so that the washer women at the Wells o' Wearie were stopped from carrying out their traditional trade on the grounds that it was not compatible with recreational use of the area. Public outcry was great at Prince Albert's plans to build a restaurant at Dunsapie, and some nineteenth-century townsfolk were very upset by vendors selling "milk and other commodities", who used to operate on the Sabbath. In common with today, the letters pages of *The Scotsman* provide a fascinating insight into the concerns of the people of Edinburgh.

By the early twentieth century, there were enough visitors in the Park between May and September to support a vendor of lemonade and biscuits, a Mr Picken, who climbed to the top every

Craft vendors at Fringe Sunday: a modern contrast to the last century when even selling milk was frowned on in the Park on a Sunday.

day. The impact of the visitors over the years may be seen in the bare rock surfaces at the summit and the well-worn path below. Countless feet have worn the grassy cover away, and the problem is gradually extending down the hill. Over the years various attempts have been made to counter the visitor erosion, including improved drainage and the laying of an artificial mesh to strengthen the grassy path that leads to the summit, but it is a difficult task.

Other visitors make use of different areas of the Park; for not everyone wants to climb to the top. The flat area of the Parade Ground has long been popular, particularly as a place for gatherings. As its name suggests, it was much in use for troop reviews, particularly in the nineteenth century, but other functions had different themes. In 1832 some sixty thousand people gathered here to discuss the Parliamentary Reform Bill. It was an impressive and orderly gathering and prompted *The Scotsman* of the day to query whether the Tories could muster so many. They went on to say "We doubt if any city in the empire can turn out a body of tradesmen so intelligent and respectable." Praise indeed!

In 1946 the British Legion held a Royal Review in the Park, as part of its anniversary celebrations, and from 1947 the Scottish

A view of the Reform Meeting held on the Parade Ground in 1832. This was drawn for The Scotsman, *and shows the presence of several buildings around the entrance to Hunter's Bog.*

VIEW OF THE GREAT REFORM MEETING AT THE KING'S PARK EDINBURGH.— APRIL 24TH 1832.

Miners combined politics and relaxation when they held their annual Gala Days here, an event that has only recently stopped. Today, one of the most popular and crowded events of the Edinburgh Festival takes place in the Park: Fringe Sunday, when several thousand people come to sample the offerings of the different theatre, music, and comic groups.

The Parade Ground provides a good starting point for various cycle and walking races round the Queen's Drive, and it is also the gathering place for many hobbyists, such as kite enthusiasts.

In addition to the more relaxing forms of recreation Holyrood offers an ideal location for exercise. Various organised events take place through the year, but individuals may also been seen on all days cycling, running or jogging through the Park. Until 1948, there were curling rinks on the south side of Duddingston Loch, and skating was once very popular here; today, the Prestonfield Golf Course, and the Royal Commonwealth Swimming Pool continue the tradition of sport.

In the past the vertical cliffs of Salisbury Crags were a popular place for rock climbing. They formed a valuable training ground, easier to reach than many of Scotland's mountain faces, especially in the days when transport was slower. This was banned for a while, because of fears for the safety of the general public (as well as fears over the climbers themselves). However, in August 1994 climbing took place again, for a trial period of a year and only in one of the Salisbury Quarries.

The special nature of Holyrood Park means that visitors can find something to suit their needs whatever they are looking for: strenuous exercise or rest and relaxation; solitary peace and quiet or all the fun of the fair. This is its unique contribution to the city of Edinburgh. It is a contribution that is well rooted into the past, and will, no doubt, continue well into the future.

(opposite) Mountaineering and cycling in the Park.

56

9 Visiting the Park Today

Holyrood Park and Arthur's Seat lie at the heart of a major city and they are a popular and easy place to visit. Anyone who goes to the Park today will quickly be aware that they are not alone, indeed the main walking routes can be crowded. Yet this is a fragile landscape, and it can be a dangerous one. It may be hard to imagine, but visitors need to take care, in order both to preserve the Park for future generations and to look after themselves. The Park today is managed by Historic Scotland and it needs the co-operation of all who visit in order to maintain its well-being.

The particular nature of its geology and botany mean that the Park is recognised as a Site of Special Scientific Interest (SSSI), and needs special measures for its protection. SSSIs are more usually associated with the countryside, well away from towns, and it may seem odd to find one at the heart of the city. This is a measure of Holyrood Park's uniqueness. It means that all who love and use the Park are in some way responsible for its up-keep. It is illegal to pick or uproot the plants of the Park, and it is also illegal to collect specimens of rock from the faces.

In addition to its natural interest, the archaeological value of the Park is such that the whole area is recognised as a Scheduled Ancient Monument. This means that the Park is specially protected, to ensure the future well-being of all the ancient remains within it. It is illegal to disturb or damage any part of the Park, whether a recognised "archaeological site", or not. Even archaeologists have to

(opposite) Samson's Ribs.

59

seek the permission of the Secretary of State for Scotland before they may carry out investigations anywhere in the Park. The use of metal detectors and other treasure-hunting equipment in the Park is also forbidden.

Every year the pressure of visitors leads to renewed erosion of the rocky paths and grassy slopes, and at times various measures are taken to stabilise and improve the main routeways. Visitors are asked to respect this, and avoid, where possible, adding to that erosion themselves. In places, paths have been improved and specially treated grass is sown as a surface. When possible, these paths should always be followed to reduce erosion problems on either side.

At the same time, though the Park makes an ideal outing for a picnic, it can be rough and wet, and there is nearly always a wind blowing at the summit. If you intend to walk it is a good idea to wear

The Radical Road.

stout, well-soled shoes for support, and you should always carry weather-proof clothing, including an extra sweater. In contrast, fire can be a serious problem, particularly in dry spells. Fires should never be lit in the Park, and all litter should be put in the litter bins or carried home. Discarded cigarettes cause a particular fire hazard and should be disposed of carefully.

Unlike most city parks, Holyrood Park has its own police force: the Royal Park Constabulary whose main task is to uphold Park regulations. The daily maintenance of the landscape is the responsibility of the Park Manager. Group events in the Park, whether they be small or large, should be notified in advance to Historic Scotland.

Occasionally, visitors to the Park may notice something unusual. The Park contains the record of many generations of

people, both visitors and those to whom it was home. From time to time relics do appear, perhaps in a new erosion face, or lying among some stones that have recently shifted. Any finds from the Park are important, because they help to tell us more about its past, and also the past of Scotland. If you should come across something that you think is archaeological, it is best to leave it undisturbed and get in touch straight away with Historic Scotland.

It is a legal requirement that any ancient object found in Scotland be reported to the proper authorities or to the police, and Historic Scotland will be happy to help with this. All such finds belong to the Crown, though the Crown does not always exert its claim. Objects are brought before a panel, the Treasure Trove Advisory Panel, which advises the Crown on where they should go and any possible reward to the finder. Generally an archaeological find is of more interest if it is possible for an archaeologist to see it *in situ*; if it is absolutely necessary to pick it up then it should be very carefully handled and the original spot where it was found should be carefully noted.

Finally, this book includes a map of the Park to help you explore and find the things that interest you. If you come into the Park by car, you will find several carparks. Please respect the parking arrangements, and drive carefully, there are always many pedestrians and they all seem to try to cross the road at the same time. At various times you will find that the Park roads may be closed to traffic: at the time of writing, there are partial Sunday road closures every week as well as occasional complete closures. If you come by bus, bike or on foot, it is important to remember that the Park is also a busy thoroughfare. Always pay attention, and try not to be distracted by the scenery.

The Park contains many walking routes, some are metalled, others grassy or gravel tracks. In addition, you can leave the path and explore across the rougher ground, though cyclists are not permitted to ride off-road. Whatever you decide to do, all of the places mentioned in this book are easy to reach and I hope that you will have much pleasure in getting to know the Park in all its different guises.

If you would like to follow up some of the information from this guide there are a number of organisations that can help.

Historic Scotland
Longmore House
Salisbury Place
Edinburgh
EH9 1SH

The Council for Scottish Archaeology
c/o National Museums of Scotland
York Buildings
Edinburgh
EH2 1JD

Edinburgh City
Archaeologist
10 Broughton Market
Old Broughton,
Edinburgh
EH3 6NU

The National Museums of Scotland
Chambers Street
Edinburgh
EH1 1JF

Scottish Natural Heritage
12 Hope Terrace
Edinburgh
EH9 2AS

Further reading

Mackenzie-Stuart AJ, *A French King at Holyrood;* John Donald, Edinburgh, 1995

Scottish Natural Heritage and British Geological Survey *Edinburgh, a landscape fashioned by geology,* Edinburgh, 1993

Stevenson RBK, *Farms and Fortifications in the King's Park, Edinburgh,* Proceedings of the Society of Antiquaries of Scotland, Edinburgh, 1987

Wright G, Adams I & Scott M, *A Guide to Holyrood Park and Arthur's Seat,* Gordon Wright Publishing, Edinburgh, 1987

Index